Bovine ESPIONAGE
and Other Stories

Compiled by Catherine Baker

Contents

OXFORD
UNIVERSITY PRESS

The Adventure of the Dented Computer

By Simon Cheshire

OK. I just have to accept it. I'm borderline genius.

There are any number of clever kids at St Egbert's School, but I can honestly say, without fear of contradiction, that I'm right up there at the top of the food chain.

My name is Sherlock Holmes. Well, no, actually my name is Kevin, but I'm giving serious thought to having it legally changed. My mum started whimpering and tugging at her collar when I announced my intention, so I think she's OK about it. She's nearly used to the deerstalker hat now. And it's a *real* deerstalker! A proper one. Exactly like Sherlock Holmes wears. It was my grandad's.

'What d'yer want wi' that dusty old thing?' he said when we found it in his attic.

It would have been far too long and complicated to start telling him all about the greatest fictional detective of all time and how I was destined to be his real-life counterpart. Grandad's not too hot on paying attention. So I said it was for a school project, and he smiled happily and patted my head, and all was fine.

Now then. My first case. It was a classic example of deductive reasoning, which I'm sure even Holmes himself would have been proud of. And a right sinister, nefarious, no-good scheme was at the very heart of this strange and baffling mystery!

I'd been on the lookout for a chance to begin my detective career for ages. I'd read all the Holmes stories twice. Except for a couple of the longer ones. And I'd taped the play versions off Radio 4 and listened to them under the bedclothes at night, so I think that counts.

It started first thing on the Monday morning after half term. We'd had to do an essay over the holiday entitled 'An Example of Great Literature'. Naturally, I'd written about *The Hound of the Baskervilles*, Holmes' most famous case. Five hundred words, Mrs Womsey had wanted, and I'd done five hundred and twelve! Wayne Banks did 'Meka-Robots Comic

Summer Special'. What a twit. Everyone else did
Harry Potter.

Except Thug Robinson. Now, with a nickname like
Thug, you can tell he wasn't the sort to go around being
nice to small puppies and having tea with the vicar, can't
you? He had a scar above his left eye from where he'd
fallen off the roof of the toilet block just before Christmas,
and if he'd ever bothered to wash his meaty hands you'd
have seen the split knuckles he'd got from demanding
dinner money with Menace. You didn't want to be in
Thug's bad books, unless you enjoyed going to the dentist.

Thug had done *War and Peace*, by some bloke called
Toystory, or something. We all just sat there, silent.
Staring at him. I'd seen that book on the bookshelf
at home. I think Mum had got it cheap somewhere.
Anyway, it wasn't something you actually *read.* It
was huge, with tiny print, boring, boring, historical,
Russian, boring.

Thug stood at the front and read out his essay. And
we were entranced. He actually made the whole thing
sound great. Mrs Womsey was speechless: 'Oh, that
was lovely, Jonathan (Thug's real name, tee hee), lovely.
Superb analysis of the book and the author. That really
was one of the very best … '

And so on. Believe me, for Mrs Womsey, that's speechless.

If it had happened once, me and the rest of 7A might have put it down to luck. Or a sudden attack of intelligence. Or copying it out of an encyclopaedia.

But he did it again on Tuesday, in French. He turned in a perfect translation of a bit in our textbook *France: The Language, The People* that was so covered in squiggly accents it looked as if someone had sneezed ink on it. Ten out of ten for Thug again.

And again on Wednesday. Chemistry. He'd not only done his homework, he'd put a formula for a new type of plastic in the margin that apparently had the Staff Room baffled for nearly a week.

It was getting worrying. Us clever kids were under threat. Well, we were always under threat from Thug Robinson, but we were more used to it being a gimme-your-cash-or-I'll-thump-you type of threat. We weren't used to having our brains challenged.

Time for me, Sherlock, to solve the mystery! I stood on a desk on Thursday break-time and announced that I would personally get to the bottom of the matter. Once the laughter had subsided, I approached Weasel Watson.

His name really was Watson. So he was destined to be my sidekick. He had no choice. He was a tall kid, and very thin. Looked like a weasel, moved like a weasel, ate like a horse that's missed its breakfast.

'So,' I concluded, after telling him about my status as the real-life Holmes and his as my personal Dr Watson. 'Are you set for adventure? Are you ready to gasp in disbelief at my powers of detection? Are you set to become my trusty companion in the fight against evil?'

'No.'

I bought him five bars of chocolate and a packet of chicken crisps from the school canteen and he changed his mind.

'Where you going to start?' he said, checking through the change in his pocket to see if he had enough for an ice-cream. 'I mean, how do we know he's not just thumping some other kid until they do his homework for him?'

'No, we'd have heard on the grapevine if that was happening. Remember the homework copying scam of 9C? Collapsed in a fortnight. No, he's getting his information from outside the school.'

Watson picked at his teeth. The bell for afternoon

lessons would be going any minute. Kids were hurrying up and down the corridor. The swotty ones were hurrying to their classrooms. The rest of them were hurrying as far away from their classrooms as possible.

'Maybe he's just got a really clever dad,' said Watson.

'Have you *seen* his dad?' I said, raising an eyebrow. 'Thug could be his clone. I doubt the man can spell his own name, let alone do a diagram of the human circulation system.'

'Well, maybe he's got a really stupid dad, but a super-fast Internet connection and loads of useful addresses?'

'No! Think, Watson, think. He's answering very specific questions, doing very specific essays. Teachers spot downloaded stuff straight off, even *our* teachers. You'd have to reorganize the information really intelligently if you were going to do that. And there's no way Thug could manage it.'

Watson thought carefully for a few moments. 'I don't get it,' he said at last.

I was delighted. Watson was turning out to be a perfect sidekick.

'Elementary, my dear Watson,' I said. 'We can deduce two important points from what we already know. Point one: Thug is stealing this information. No kid we know could produce homework of this quality. No adult would supply him with it, either willingly or unwillingly. They hate him more than we do. But! Point two: he must be getting the information from a source *connected* to the school because it matches up so spot-on with the homework we're being set. His source is therefore likely to be someone who *knows* what the questions are in advance.'

Watson's jaw dropped. He really was ideal sidekick material, this kid.

'A teacher?' he gasped.

'That is a distinct possibility,' I said. At this point, Sherlock Holmes would have popped his curly pipe into his mouth and puffed away mysteriously. I'd tried using a cardboard cut-out pipe before, but it didn't look right. I'd decided to ditch the idea. Besides, smoking was a dirty habit and I didn't want to set a bad example for Watson.

The bell went for lessons. During Maths, I scribbled a few notes in the back of my exercise book and gave a good think to the problem of what to do next.

Holmes had his Baker Street Irregulars, so I'd have my St Egbert's Irregulars. The Baker Street version was a bunch of kids who went out scouting around on

Holmes' behalf, forming a secret network of eyes that could keep watch on suspicious persons.

So the following break-time, I enlisted the help of a gang of eager tinies from the Reception class. 'Follow Thug Robinson,' I told them. 'Watch his every move. You are my secret network of eyes.'

Twenty-four hours later, they reported back. Three of them had taken me literally, and had to be collected by angry parents from off Thug's doorstep. Five had got the wrong Robinson, and told me all about Sally Robinson's dolly that said 'mama'. The rest of them turned up and said they'd seen Thug captured by aliens from a pirate ship, definitely, true, honest, and could they have the pound coins I'd promised them now?

So much for that. If you want a job doing properly, do it yourself!

I collected Watson and off we went. Thug wasn't a difficult person to trail. If you lost sight of his chunky frame in the crowd, you could always follow the sound of arms being twisted.

We managed to keep track of his movements for over half the following week, without getting a single significant clue. Everywhere he went, people got out of his way if they saw him coming or, if they didn't see him coming, soon wished they could get out of his way.

Until!

It was nearly going-home time, Wednesday. They were repainting the school gates (following an unfortunate incident with a bag of jam doughnuts and Sickly O'Sullivan's stomach), so we all had to leave via the side exit that the older kids from the senior school usually used.

I grabbed Watson by the collar and dragged him into the shadows by the Modern Languages block.

'What?' he demanded, spraying a mouthful of crumbs everywhere. 'I nearly dropped my pasty.'

'Look!' I said, putting on the intense, hawk-like expression that had taken me hours to perfect in the bathroom mirror. 'Look who Thug's with!'

Thug was talking to a very smart boy with very neat hair and very small glasses. The boy was chatting amiably, and so was Thug.

'Who's that then?' said Watson.

'I have absolutely no idea,' I said. I was pretty sure I'd seen him in school assemblies being presented with prizes. 'I think he's in the year above us. Or possibly the year above that.'

'And why does it matter?' said Watson.

'Oh, for goodness' sake, Watson,' I sighed. 'Look at them! Thug's being friendly! He doesn't do that any other time, does he? That kid could be significant.'

I waited for Thug to be on his way. Then, as the boy approached, I sprang from the shadows, pulling Watson after me. Sherlock Holmes was a master of disguise, possessing an uncanny ability which aided him many times in his quest for the truth.

I put on a thick Scottish accent. 'Och aye, hallo!'

The boy stopped and blinked at me nervously. 'Hallo!' he said. 'Do I know you? Sorry, chaps, must dash, I'm late for choir practice.' He had a very posh voice, too. I had an inkling as to who he was now. I just couldn't recall his name.

'Aye, laddy,' I said, 'just a wee word. Ma friend here and I were jus' thinking, was that Thug Robinson you were talkin' to back there? Only I said that a lad like yourself,' errr ... Angus, a lad like yourself wouldnae be ... '

'My name's not Angus,' said the boy, 'it's Maurice.'

Of course! Mega-Maurice! The brainiest pupil in the school! The kid was a legend. He was the one who'd rewired all the computers in the IT room, after they'd been cleaned of a virus the year before.

'So, umm, how do you know Thug Robinson, hoots mon[1]?' I said.

'He's our cleaning lady at home,' said Maurice.

Watson's eyes widened. Mine narrowed.

'Well, not "lady", of course,' said Maurice. 'But he pops in and tidies up every day after school. He's pretty good at it and charges a very reasonable rate. He does my room a treat. I wouldn't have thought him capable, personally, but it just goes to show there's good in everyone.'

'And, er, he simply volunteered for this, did he?' I said.

'Yes,' said Maurice. 'He lives next door to us. I had to baby-sit the nasty little worm during half term. He wouldn't stop tampering with my PC. But you can't print or email without a password, so he didn't do any damage, fortunately. Anyway, I happened to mention that our last cleaning lady had run off to join the circus and all of a sudden he was nice as pie and said he'd do it. I'd thought he was a right horror at first, but I've got to admit I was wrong.'

'Och, aye,' I said, 'he's a great wee laddy.'

'Look,' said Maurice crossly, 'why are you so interested in who cleans my room? Are you after something? And what's with the stupid fake accent? Eh?'

We were faced with extremely awkward questions,

---

[1] Scottish expression used to get someone's attention.

so Watson and I did what any crime-fighting duo in our position would have done. We ran away.

Apart from a stop-over for Watson to get a hamburger, it was full speed back to my house all the way. I was feeling rather chuffed.

'I'm feeling rather confused,' said Watson, stuffing down the last of his sesame bun.

'On the contrary, Watson,' I said confidently. 'Things become clearer every minute.'

'Clearer how exactly?' said Watson, after a tum-loosening belch.

'All we have to do now is infiltrate Thug Robinson's room.'

I won't go into Watson's reaction. Let's just say it wasn't polite. But it was vital to get a look at Thug's room, to confirm my suspicions, or at least to give me a few final clues to the whole story.

'If I'm right,' I said, 'we'll find an old and clunky computer in there.'

Getting into Thug's house proved easier than I'd imagined. We waited until we knew Thug was out frightening toddlers in the park, and swooped. I rang the doorbell.

Thug's dad appeared, scratching his bum. He had

a big, grubby plaster stuck to his forehead. He was completely fooled by our blue overalls, fake ID cards, and false moustaches.

'Is everyone from the electric company as short as you two?' he said, scratching his leg.

'Oh, yes, sir,' I said. 'Requirement of the job. In case we need to squeeze into any confined spaces. Now, we've had reports of dangerous wiring in this street, so we're having to check every premise, especially the upstairs.'

'Be my guest,' said Thug's dad, scratching his head. 'But I'm not doin' you a cup of tea.'

Thug's room was disgusting. No, worse than disgusting. We didn't dare touch anything for fear of contracting a disease.

But!

The vital clue was there, just as I'd expected. Sitting on a chipped sideboard that was overflowing with stained T-shirts. The PC was not only old and clunky, it was – and this was the decider – dented on top. There was a sharp V-shape in its CPU case, which had split the machine's CD-ROM tray, making it unusable.

I switched the computer on and it wheezed into life. From the pocket of my overalls I produced a floppy disk[1] and copied its contents on to the hard drive.

---

[1] A floppy disk was a device for storing information, similar to a USB stick. It was mainly used with computers in the 1980s and 1990s.

'What are you *doing*?' hissed Watson.

'On this disk is the virus they cleaned off the computers in the IT room last year. Sherlock Holmes collected odd bits of kit, and so do I. It scrambles files so they look OK but read like gobbledegook.'

Watson hissed a few more questions at me, but when did you ever hear of a detective revealing the plot before the final scene? Quite!

We reassured Thug's dad that his wiring was absolutely fine and made a hasty retreat. Just in time too – Thug was coming down the street as we dashed off in the opposite direction.

Right. Final scene.

Class, the next morning. We all hand in our homework on the life of Charles Dickens. Thug gives his to Mrs Womsey with his now-usual smug grin. She flicks through it.

'Jonathan,' she said quietly. 'This is nonsense. This is gobbledegook. Dickens was not a puff adder. Neither was he French, nor the inventor of the nuclear explosion. You've been doing so well lately, and now you've gone back to your old ways.'

Thug looked shocked. Watson looked amazed. I looked pretty darn cool.

Of course, after that, Thug's brief reign as class brainbox was over. His homework plummeted back into the gutter from whence it came and good riddance.

'How?' said Watson, admiringly. 'Why, when, where, and what?'

'Elementary,' I said calmly. 'Thug sees Mega-Maurice's room in half term. More specifically, his PC, packed with all the brilliant, teacher-pleasing homework he's ever done. Maurice is a year or two ahead of us, therefore he's already done all the homework that we're being set now. Thug spots an opportunity to cheat. But, oh dear, he's a right thicko and parts of Maurice's PC are passworded. He can't print or email Maurice's old homework. He can download it, though; even he can manage that. But, oh dear again, his own PC is dented. His CD-ROM is broken. He can't copy lots of files. All he can copy is one floppy disk's worth at a time. And if he's going to do that, he needs regular access to Maurice's computer. So he volunteers to be a cleaning lady, and every day, while Maurice isn't looking, he copies another disk's-worth of info, whatever is that night's homework. He takes it home, prints it out, or copies it down in his own scrawly handwriting, and bingo. He's top of the class.'

'And the virus means that every file he tries to copy now will come out scrambled,' said Watson.

I sat back and gazed out of the window. To have a mind as brilliant as mine is a gift, and I intend to share that gift with the world. I'm thinking of taking up the violin.

Rincemangle, the Gnome of Even Moor

By Terry Pratchett

Once upon a time there was a gnome who lived in a hollow tree on Even Moor, the strange mysterious land to the north of Blackbury. His name was Rincemangle and as far as he knew he was the only gnome left in the world.

He didn't look very gnome-like. He wore a pointed hat, of course, because gnomes do; but apart from that he wore a shabby mouse-skin suit and a rather smelly overcoat made from old moleskins. He lived on nuts and berries and the remains of picnics, and birds' eggs when he could get them. It wasn't a very joyful life.

One day he was sitting in his hollow tree, gnawing a hazelnut. It was pouring with rain and the tree leaked. Rincemangle thought he was getting nasty twinges in his joints.

'Blow this for a lark,' he said. 'I'm wet through and fed up.'

An owl who lived in the tree next door heard him and flew over. 'You should go out and see the world,' he said. 'There're more places than Even Moor.' And he told him stories about the streets of Blackbury and places even further away, where the sun always shone and the seas were blue. Actually, they weren't very accurate, because the owl had heard them from a blackbird, who had heard them from a swallow, who had gone there for his holidays, but they were enough to get Rincemangle feeling very restive.

In less time than it takes to tell, he had packed his few possessions in a handkerchief. 'I'm off!' he cried. 'To places where the sun always shines! How far did you say they were?'

'Er,' said the owl, who hadn't the faintest idea, 'about a couple of miles, I expect. Perhaps a bit more.'

'Cheerio then,' said Rincemangle. 'If you could read I'd send you a postcard, if I could write.'

He scrambled down the tree and set off.

When Rincemangle the gnome set off down the road to Blackbury he really didn't know how far it was.

It was raining, and he soon got fed up.

After a while he came to a layby. There was a
lorry parked there while the driver ate his lunch and
Rincemangle, who had often watched lorries go past
his tree, climbed up a tyre and looked for somewhere
warm to sleep under the tarpaulin.

The lorry was full of cardboard boxes. He nibbled
one and found it was full of horrible tins. They weren't
even comfortable to sleep on. But he did eventually
drop off, just as the lorry set off again to Blackbury.
When Rincemangle woke up, it was very dark in
the box, and there was a lot of banging about going
on; then that stopped, and after waiting until all the
sounds had died away, he peered cautiously through
the hole.

The first thing he saw was another gnome.

'Hullo,' said the gnome. 'Is there much interesting in
there? It looks like another load of baked beans to me.
Here, help me get a tin out.'

Together they gnawed at the box until one tin rolled
out. The box was on a high shelf, but the other gnome
had got up by climbing it rather like a mountaineer.
They lowered the tin down on a piece of thread.

'My name's Featherhead,' said the gnome. 'You're new here, aren't you? Just up from the country?'

'I thought I was the only gnome in the world,' said Rincemangle.

'Oh, there're a lot of us here. Who wants to live in a hollow tree when you can live in a department store like this?'

Talking and rolling the tin along in front of them, they crept out of the storeroom and set off. The department store was closed for the night, of course, but a few lights had been left on. There was a rather nasty moment when they had to hide from the lady who cleaned the floors but, after a long haul up some stairs, Rincemangle arrived at the gnomes' home.

The gnomes had built themselves a home under the floorboards between the toy shop and the do-it-yourself department, though they had – er – borrowed quite a lot of railway track from the toy shop and built a sort of underground railway all the way to the restaurant. They even had a telephone rigged up between the colony and the gnomes who lived in the Gents' Suiting department two floors down.

All this came as a great shock to Rincemangle, of course. When he arrived with his new friend Featherhead, pushing the baked bean tin in front of them, he felt quite out of place. The gnomes lived in small cardboard houses under the floorboards, with holes drilled through the ceiling to let the light in. Featherhead rolled the tin into his house and shut the trapdoor.

'Well, this is a cut above the old hollow tree,' said Rincemangle, looking round.

'Everyone's in the restaurant, I expect,' said Featherhead. 'There's about three hundred gnomes live here, you know. My word, I think it's very odd, you living out in all weathers! Most gnomes have lived indoors for years!'

He led Rincemangle along the floor, through a hole in a brick wall and along a very narrow ledge. It was the lift, he explained. Of course, the gnomes had managed to use the big lift, but they'd rigged up a smaller one at the side of the shaft. It was driven by clockwork.

They arrived in the Gents' Suiting department after a long ride down the dark shaft. It was brightly lit, and several gnomes were working a giant sewing machine.

'Good evening!' said one, bustling up, rubbing his hands. 'Hullo Featherhead – what can I do for you?'

'My friend here in the moleskin trousers –' began Featherhead, '– can't you make him something natty in tweed? We can't have a gnome who looks like he's just stepped out of a mushroom!'

The gnomish tailors worked hard. They made Rincemangle a suit out of a square of cloth in a pattern book and there was enough over for a spare waistcoat.

Featherhead led him back down under the floorboards and they went on to the Toy department, where most of the gnomes spent the night (they slept when the store was open during the day).

All the lights were on. Two gnomes were racing model cars around the display stands. Two teams of gnomes had unrolled one of those big football games and had started playing, while the crowd squeaked with excitement.

'Don't any human beings ever come down here at night?' asked Rincemangle, who was a bit shocked. 'I mean, you don't keep look-outs or anything!'

'Oh, no one comes here after the cleaners have gone home,' said Featherhead. 'We have the place to ourselves.'

But they didn't. You see, the store people had noticed how food disappeared and how things had been moved around in the night. They were sensible and didn't believe in gnomes. So they had bought a cat.

Rincemangle saw it first. He looked up from the football game and saw a big green eye watching them through the partly open door. He didn't know it was a cat, but it looked like a fox, and he knew what foxes were like.

'Run for your lives!' he bellowed.

Everyone saw the cat as it pushed open the door. With shrill cries of alarm, several gnomes rolled back the carpet and opened the trapdoor to their underground homes, but they were too late. The cat trotted in and stared at them.

'Stand still now,' hissed Rincemangle. 'He'll get you if you move!'

Fortunately, perhaps because of the way he said it, the gnomes stood still. Rincemangle thought quickly, and then ran to one of the toy cars the gnomes had been using. As the cat bounded after him he drove away.

He wasn't very good at steering, but managed to drive right out of the Toy department before crashing the car into a display. He jumped out and climbed the stem of a potted plant just as the cat dashed up.

Rincemangle the gnome climbed right up the potted plant just as the cat came scampering towards him. From the topmost leaf he was able to jump on to a shelf, and he ran and hid behind a stack of china plates – knocking quite a few down in the process, I'm sorry to say.

After half an hour or so the cat got fed up and wandered off, and he was able to climb down.

When he got back to the gnome home under the floorboards, the place was in uproar. Some families were gathering their possessions together, and several noisy meetings were going on.

He found Featherhead packing his belongings into an old tea caddy. 'Oh hullo,' he said. 'I say, that was pretty clever of you, leading the cat away like that!'

'What are you doing?'

'Well, we can't stay here now they've got a cat, can we?' said Featherhead.

But it was even worse than that, because very soon the night-watchman, who usually stayed downstairs, came up and saw all the broken plates on the floor, and he called the police.

All the next day the gnomes tried to sleep, and when the store emptied for the night the Head Gnomes called them all together. They decided that the only thing to do was to leave the store. But where could they go?

Rincemangle stood up and said, 'Why don't you go back and live in the country? That's where gnomes used to live.'

They were all shocked. One fat gnome said, 'But the food here is so marvellous. There're wild animals in the country, so I've heard tell, that are worse than cats even!'

'Besides,' someone else said, 'how would we get there? All three hundred of us? It's miles and miles away!'

Just then two gnomes burst in, dragging a saucer full of blue powder. It smelt odd, they said. They'd found it in the restaurant.

Rincemangle sniffed at it. 'It's poison,' he said. 'They think we're mice! I tell you, if we don't leave soon we'll all be killed.'

Featherhead said, 'I think he's right. But how can we leave? Think of the roads we'd have to cross, for one thing!'

As the days passed, things got worse and worse for the gnomes. Apart from the cat, there were night-watchmen patrolling the store after everyone had gone home, and the gnomes hardly dared to show themselves.

But they couldn't think of a way to leave. None of them fancied walking through the city with all its dangers. There were the lorries that delivered goods every day, but only a few brave gnomes were prepared to be a stowaway on them – and, besides, no one knew where they would stop.

'We will have to take so much with us!' moaned the Head Gnome, sitting sadly on an empty cotton reel. 'String, and cloth, and all sorts of things. Food, too. A lot of the younger gnomes wouldn't survive for five minutes in the country otherwise. We've had such an easy life here, you see.'

Rincemangle scratched his head. 'I suppose so, but you'll have to give it up sooner or later. Where's Featherhead?'

Featherhead, the gnome Rincemangle was staying with, had led a raid on the book section to see if there were any books about living in the country.

Towards dawn, a party of tired gnomes came back, dragging a big paper bag.

'We were almost spotted by the night-watchman,' muttered Featherhead. 'We got a few books, though.'

There was one in the sack that had nothing to do with the country. Rincemangle looked at it for a long time.

'*Teach Yourself to Drive*,' he said. 'Hmmm.' He opened it with some difficulty and saw a large picture of the controls of a car. He didn't say anything for a long time.

Finally the Head Gnome said, 'It's very interesting, but I hardly think you're big enough to drive anything!'

'No,' said Rincemangle. 'But perhaps ... Featherhead, can you show me where the lorries are parked at night? I've got an idea.'

Early the next evening, the two gnomes reached the large underground car park where the store's lorries were parked. The journey had taken them quite a long time because they took turns at dragging the book on driving behind them.

And it took them all night to examine the lorry. When they arrived back at the Toy department, they were very tired and covered in oil.

Rincemangle called the gnomes together. 'I think we can leave here and take things with us,' he said, 'but it will be rather tricky. We'll have to drive a lorry, you see.'

He drew diagrams to explain. A hundred gnomes would turn the steering wheel by pulling on ropes, while fifty would be in charge of the gear lever. Other groups would push the pedals when necessary, and one gnome would hang from the driving mirror and give commands through a megaphone.

'It looks quite straightforward,' said Rincemangle. 'To me it looks as though driving just involves pushing and pulling things at the right time.'

An elderly gnome got up and said nervously, 'I'm not sure about all this. I'm sure there must be more to driving than that.'

But a lot of the younger gnomes were very enthusiastic, and so the idea took hold.

For the rest of the week the gnomes were very busy. Some stole bits of string from the hardware department, and several times they visited the lorries at night to take measurements and try to find out how it worked. Meanwhile, the older gnomes rolled their possessions down through the store until they were piled up in the ceiling of the lorry garage.

A handpicked party of intrepid mountaineering gnomes found out where the lorry keys were kept (high up on a hook in a little office). Rincemangle, meanwhile, studied road maps and wondered what the Highway Code was.

At last the day came for moving.

'We've got to work fast,' said Rincemangle, when they heard the last assistant leave the building. 'Come on – now!'

While the gnomes lowered their possessions through the garage roof on to the back of the lorry, Rincemangle and an advance party of young gnomes squeezed into the cab through a hole by the brake pedal.

Inside it was – to them – like being in a big empty hall. The steering wheel seemed very big and far too high up.

The gnomes formed themselves into a human pyramid and, by standing on the topmost gnome's back, Rincemangle managed to throw a line over the steering wheel. Soon they had several rope ladders rigged up and could set to work.

They planned to steer by two ropes tied to the wheel, with fifty gnomes hanging on to each one. While this was being sorted out, other gnomes built a sort of wooden platform up against the windscreen, just big enough for Rincemangle to stand and give orders through a megaphone.

Other gnomes came in and were sent to their positions by Featherhead. Before long, the cab was festooned with rope ladders, pulleys and fragile wooden platforms, and these in turn were covered with gnomes hanging on to levers and lengths of thread.

The big moment came when the ignition key was hauled up and shoved into its keyhole by two muscular gnomes. They gave a twist and some lights came on.

'Right,' said Rincemangle, looking down at the waiting crowds. 'Well, this is going to be a tricky business, so let's get started right away.'

Featherhead joined him on the platform and hauled up the *Teach Yourself to Drive* book and a street map of Blackbury.

'On the word "Go", the Starter Button party will give it a good press and – er – the Accelerator Pedal squad will press the pedal briefly,' Rincemangle said uncertainly. 'The gnomes working the clutch and gear lever will stand by. Go!'

Of course, it didn't work as simply as that. It took quite some time before the gnomes found out how to start up properly. But at last the engine was going, making the cab boom like a gong.

'Headlights on! Clutch down! First gear!' Rincemangle shouted above the din. There were several ghastly crashes and the great lorry rolled forward.

'Here, what about the garage doors?' shouted Featherhead.

The lorry rolled onwards. There was a loud bang and it was out in the street.

'Turn left!' shouted Rincemangle hoarsely. 'Now straighten up!'

For several minutes the cab was full of shouts and bangs as the gnomes pushed and pulled on the controls. The lorry wove from side to side and went up on the pavement several times, but at least it kept going. Rincemangle even felt bold enough to order a gear change.

Through the dark streets of Blackbury the lorry

swayed and rumbled, occasionally bouncing off lamp-posts. Every now and again there was a horrible clonk as it changed gear.

Steering was the big difficulty. By the time the gnomes down below had heard Rincemangle's order, it was usually too late. It was a good job there were no other vehicles on the road at that time of night, or there would have been a very nasty accident.

They blundered through the traffic lights and into Blackbury High Street, knocking a piece off a pillar box.

Featherhead was staring into the great big mirror high above them that showed what traffic was behind. 'There's a car behind with a big blue flashing light on it,' he said conversationally. 'Listen! It's making a siren noise.'

'Very decorative, I'm sure,' said Rincemangle, who wasn't really listening. 'Look lively down below! It's a straight road out of town now, so change into top gear.'

There was a thud and a crash, but the gnomes were getting experienced now and the lorry whizzed away, still weaving from side to side.

'The car with the flashing lights keeps trying to overtake us,' said Featherhead. 'Gosh! We nearly hit it that time!'

He craned up and had another look. 'There's two human beings in peaked caps inside it,' he added. 'Gosh! They look furious!'

'I expect someone has got a little angry because of all those lamp-posts we knocked down. I don't think we were supposed to,' said Rincemangle.

Unfortunately, while he said this, he didn't look where they were going. The lorry rumbled off the road and straight through a hedge. The field behind it was ploughed, and the gnomes had to hang on tightly as they were jolted around in the cab.

The police car screeched to a halt and the two policemen started running across the field after them, shouting.

The lorry went through another hedge and frightened a herd of cows.

Rincemangle peered through the window. There was a wood ahead, and behind that the heather-clad slopes of Even Moor started climbing up towards the sky.

'Prepare to abandon lorry!' he shouted. They plunged into a wood and the lorry stopped dead in the middle of a bramble thicket. It was suddenly very quiet.

Then there was a very busy five minutes as the gnomes unloaded their possessions from the back of the lorry. By the time the policemen arrived, there was not a gnome to be seen. Rincemangle and Featherhead were sitting high up on a bramble branch and watched as the men wandered round the abandoned lorry, scratching their heads. After poking around inside the cab and finding the little ropes and ladders, they wandered away, arguing.

When they had gone, the gnomes crept out of their hiding places and gathered round Rincemangle.

'Even Moor is only a few hundred yards away,' he said. 'Let's spend the day hidden here and we can be up there tonight!'

The gnomes lit fires and settled down to cook breakfast. Many of them were wondering what it would be like to live in the country again after so long in the town. A lot of the little ones, of course – I mean, even littler than the average gnome – were rather looking forward to it. But they all knew that there was going to be a lot of hard work before them.

Early next morning, a poacher, coming home for

breakfast, told his wife he'd seen a lot of little lights climbing up the slopes of the moor. She didn't believe him, but perhaps you will.

Stationery Is Never Stationary

By Morris Gleitzman

'Come on, both of you,' said Mum. 'We'll be late. Jack, switch that game off and get your shoes on. If we don't leave soon, it won't be worth going.'

It's never worth going, thought Jack gloomily. *Big family get-togethers should be banned.*

While he tied his shoes, Jack imagined a world without Christmas, Easter, birthdays, engagements, weddings, babies, anniversaries, funerals, public holidays, exam results, holiday videos, new houses, overseas trips, footy grand finals and hearing about people's operations.

Heaven.

Because that would be a world where big families wouldn't have any reason to get together. And innocent dads wouldn't feel like losers just because of their jobs.

'Amazing,' said Dad, still on the couch gazing at his laptop. 'There's a company in Japan that makes teflon-coated staples.'

'Archie,' Mum said to him, her voice loud with exasperation. 'We'll be late.'

'Do we have to go?' said Jack to Mum, like he always did.

'Yes,' said Mum, like she always did. 'Uncle Pete wants us all to see his new home entertainment set-up. Plus it's Aunty Sue's birthday tomorrow, my cousin Niall's just back from Venezuela, Aunty Anthea wants us to meet her new boyfriend and we have to talk about where we're going to have Christmas. Archie, if you don't switch that computer off, I'll brain you with it.'

In the car on the way there, Jack felt miserable like he always did when he and Mum and Dad got together with the rest of the family.

Then he made a vow.

This time he'd try even harder. This time he'd do it. This time he'd make the rest of the family respect Dad's job.

In the driver's seat, Dad turned to Mum. 'You know what this means,' he said.

'What?' said Mum.

'That crowd in Japan must have a staple remover that can handle teflon,' said Dad.

'Concentrate on the road,' said Mum.

Jack concentrated on being determined and hopeful. He was ten now and he was sure he could do it. Simple, really.

All he had to do was make Uncle Pete and the others understand that working in a stationery shop was one of the most important jobs in the world.

Uncle Pete opened the front door, his big suntanned face beaming. 'The slack mob have arrived,' he called over his shoulder.

'We're only a few minutes late,' said Mum.

'Doesn't matter,' said Uncle Pete. 'We're just glad you're here. We've run out of paperclips.'

Uncle Pete clearly thought this was hilarious.

Jack thought about taking Uncle Pete to Japan, so Uncle Pete could discover the advantages of teflon-coated staples. In particular how they're less painful when someone staples your mouth shut.

He decided not to.

Dad was gazing at Uncle Pete with a nervous smile.

Mum was rolling her eyes. 'Thought you top barristers were meant to be witty and original,' she said, kissing Uncle Pete on the cheek.

Give me half an hour, said Jack silently to Uncle Pete, *and you'll be gazing at Dad with new respect.*

'I don't do original at weekends,' said Uncle Pete. 'This lot can't afford it. I save it for the people who pay me six grand a day. Probably the same with you, eh, Archie? You probably don't bring your best manila folders home on weekends.'

'Not often,' said Dad. 'Though actually these days the best folders are made from hot-milled cellulose.'

The rest of the family were around the pool. They raised their glasses to Mum and Dad and Jack.

'Rob's just telling us about the hospital he's building in Africa,' said Uncle Pete.

'I'm not actually building it myself,' said Uncle Rob modestly. 'Just arranging the finance.'

Jack waited patiently while Uncle Rob spent the next ten minutes telling them exactly how. Finally he finished.

Before Jack could get started with what he wanted to say, Aunty Anthea butted in.

'Rakesh is a digital microchip designer,' she said, giving her new boyfriend a squeeze. 'He's just had a fantastic breakthrough. He's invented a microchip that can be inserted into bananas on trees, and when each banana gets ripe, it sends a text to the farmer.'

Everyone murmured in an impressed way.

Rakesh shrugged modestly.

Jack opened his mouth to say his piece, but Uncle Pete spoke first. 'What about mangoes?' he said to Rakesh. 'I love mangoes.'

'I'm working on that,' said Rakesh.

Everyone murmured again, in an even more impressed way.

'The plum industry in Venezuela's been having a few problems,' said Mum's cousin Niall before Jack could get a word in. 'That's why I was over there. Helping them eradicate the sap-sucking fruit moth. We did it with genetic modification. Quite easy really, but don't tell that to the Nobel Prize committee.'

'South American fruit industry,' said Aunty Sue, snapping her fingers. 'Didn't you have something to do with that, Pete?'

Say no, begged Jack silently.

Uncle Pete shrugged even more modestly than Rakesh had.

'Just helped out a few of the growers,' he said. 'Twenty thousand indigenous Impala people from the northern rainforests. They were being victimized by an oil company who wanted them off their land.'

'How terrible,' said Mum.

'Oil company was burning their homes,' said Uncle Pete. 'Plus it wouldn't accept their supermarket discount coupons at petrol stations. I got it all sorted out for them in the International Court of Justice.'

Everyone murmured in a glad sort of way.

Except Jack. He was starting to feel weak and defeated, like he always did at big family get-togethers.

It was happening again.

He couldn't even get a word in.

'Saw you interviewing the prime minister on telly,' said Aunty Sue to Mum. 'Good job.'

Mum shrugged modestly.

At least when Mum looks modest, thought Jack, *she means it*.

'What about you?' said Mum to Aunty Sue. 'Heard on the grapevine they want you to run that new university in Singapore.'

Aunty Sue gave a wry smile. 'Can't see it happening,' she said. 'They want me to stay on as Vice-Chancellor of the uni here as well. I'd be flying up and down every second day.'

'Come on,' said Aunty Anthea. 'Get real. I'm the chairman of Qantas. I can get you discount fares.'

Everyone laughed fondly.

Except Jack, who felt like pushing everyone into the pool.

'What about you, Archie?' said Uncle Pete to Dad. 'What's new for you at work?'

Jack had been dreading this. He felt sick.

Dad thought for a moment, chewing his lip. Then his face brightened. 'There's a very interesting range of non-toxic highlighters that's just come in,' he said. 'Oh, and we've finally found some price labels that don't leave sticky marks on the pens.'

There was a long silence.

Jack watched in agony as the others just looked

at Dad.

It was now or never.

'Dad saved several hundred lives last week,' said Jack.

Everybody looked at Jack, surprised. And puzzled. And clearly not believing him.

Specially Dad.

'It's true,' said Jack. 'Don't be modest, Dad. Tell them how many notebooks you sold last week.'

Still puzzled, Dad had a think. 'Ten maybe,' he said. 'And quite a few post-its.'

'There you go,' said Jack. 'Imagine how many disasters would've happened if those people hadn't been able to write themselves notes. *Remember to turn the gas off*. There's a few houses blown up for a start. *Feed the dog*. Pets can turn really nasty when their blood-sugar level drops. *Don't leave the chainsaw where the kids can play with it*. See what I mean?'

Jack looked around at the staring family members.

They didn't seem to see what he meant.

'Sticky tape,' he said desperately. 'Imagine what would happen if people's glasses snapped while they were driving and they didn't have sticky tape. Carnage on the roads.'

Uncle Pete and the others were starting to frown and glance at Mum and Dad.

Jack kept going. 'Pens with sparkly ink,' he said. 'They can prevent wars. If the leaders of two countries are having a border dispute, a birthday card signed in sparkly ink can make all the difference.'

Mum put her arm on Jack's shoulder. 'That's enough, love,' she said. 'It's a good point, but you've made it.'

Jack could see from everyone's faces that he hadn't made it very well.

Even Dad didn't look convinced.

'Bit of advice, Jack,' said Uncle Pete. 'From the legal world. You're talking about things that haven't happened. People don't care about things that haven't happened.'

Aunty Sue and the others nodded.

Jack went into the house.

You're wrong, Uncle Pete, he thought. People can care a lot about things that haven't happened. For example, there's an important thing that hasn't happened right now. Nobody's patting Dad on the back and saying,

'Wow, Archie, we hadn't realized how important and interesting your job is.' That definitely hasn't happened.

Jack glanced out the window, just to make sure.

Nope, not happening.

'Wow, Pete,' said Aunty Anthea. 'We hadn't realized how expensive and impressive your new home entertainment set-up is.'

The rest of the family murmured in agreement.

Uncle Pete grinned proudly.

Jack, who'd followed the family down the steps, had to admit it was impressive. A room specially excavated under Uncle Pete's house with a massive TV screen and a pile of high-tech equipment and about sixteen speakers.

'If you're going to do something,' said Pete, 'you might as well do it properly. I mean, Archie, you wouldn't sell a ring-binder with only one ring, would you?'

Dad shook his head.

Jack saw him struggling to think of something to say, like he always did. Jack felt a pang in his tummy, like he always did.

'Hope you've increased your home contents insurance,' said Mum to Uncle Pete. 'You must have spent a packet in here.'

'Only about a hundred and twenty grand,' said Uncle Pete. 'And I don't have to worry about burglars because this baby's got a state-of-the-art security system.'

He picked up the biggest and most expensive-looking remote Jack had ever seen, and pressed one of the buttons. With an expensive-sounding clunk, a metal door slid shut across the doorway they'd come through.

'Impressive,' said Aunty Anthea's new boyfriend, Rakesh. 'Controlled by an 87659SLK Quad, I bet. Very fine chip.'

'I told them I wanted the best,' said Uncle Pete.

As he said this, several more clunks, much louder, came from above their heads.

'What was that?' said Aunty Sue, looking alarmed.

Jack saw that Uncle Pete was looking alarmed too. But only for a moment. Then he grinned.

'Must be the soil settling,' he said. 'The builders cracked a pool pipe when they were excavating down here and it started leaking this week, so I got them to dig under the pool and fix it.'

'They were terrified,' said Aunty Sue. 'Pete said he'd

have them in the International Court of Justice if they weren't finished by Friday.'

Uncle Pete rolled his eyes. 'Not the International Court,' he said. 'Just the High Court.'

Jack was about to comment that the sticky tape Dad sold could have fixed the problem, when he noticed water running down the wall behind Uncle Pete. It was trickling in through the ventilation grilles.

'Excuse me, Uncle Pete,' he said, pointing.

But Uncle Pete didn't hear. He was busy talking to the others. 'The walls are packed with clay specially imported from Bolivia,' said Uncle Pete. 'Bolivian clay is brilliant for keeping noise out. Absolutely no sound gets through it.'

'I was able to advise Pete about that,' said Niall. 'My work with the acoustic properties of Bolivian clay in Third World concert halls won me a Guns 'N' Roses Foundation Research Fellowship.'

The others murmured in an impressed way.

'My research methodology was quite simple,' said Niall. 'I didn't have a shower for three weeks in Bolivia and discovered I couldn't hear my noisy neighbours due to the build-up of clay in my ears.'

The others murmured in an even more impressed way.

Then Mum noticed something. 'Pete,' she said. 'Why is the floor wet?'

'It's because of that water running down the wall,' said Jack.

Uncle Pete turned, and his eyes went wide. Water was coming in through the ventilation grilles even faster now.

'Jeez,' said Uncle Pete. 'That shouldn't be happening.'

Other family members murmured in agreement.

'Quick,' said Uncle Pete. 'Turn all this gear off.'

He and Uncle Rob dashed around, switching all the equipment off.

By the time they'd finished, water was gushing in. It was up to Jack's ankles.

'Everybody out,' said Uncle Pete.

He stabbed a button on the remote. The door stayed closed. He pushed several more buttons. The door didn't open. He pounded all the buttons. Nothing.

'That's the one problem with the 87659SLK Quad,'

said Rakesh. 'Doesn't work if it gets damp.'

Uncle Pete sloshed over to the door and dried as much of it as he could with his shirt tail. He wiped the remote as well. Then he pressed all the buttons again. And again. And again.

The door still didn't move.

The water was nearly up to their knees.

'Don't panic,' said Mum to Jack. 'It'll start draining away in a sec.'

'No, it won't,' said Uncle Pete. 'This room is completely sealed. I didn't want any humidity warping my turntable.'

'I'll ring for help,' said Aunty Anthea, fumbling with her phone. 'What's the number for the State Emergency Service?'

'Don't bother,' said Niall. 'Bolivian clay totally blocks phone signals. It's got tiny particles of mica in it. The CIA use it in all their buildings.'

The family members all stared at Uncle Pete.

'I had to use it,' protested Uncle Pete. 'Phone signals can affect blu-ray picture quality.'

'Why's the air in here starting to smell stale?' said

Uncle Rob.

Aunty Sue sniffed. 'Shouldn't be,' she said. 'It's air-conditioned.'

'I put in a three-phase industrial-quality air-management system with anti-static pollen filters,' said Uncle Pete.

He waded over to the only ventilation grille that didn't have water gushing out of it, reached up and held his hand in front of it.

'Poop,' he said. 'The water must have shorted the air-con motors.'

Aunty Sue gave a sob.

The water was over their knees.

And Jack's waist. He looked frantically around the room. No windows. No more doors. Not even a fire escape.

'We'll have to dig our way out,' said Uncle Rob. 'I've seen it done. The workers at the hospital in Africa had to do it when they were building the staff squash court and some scaffolding collapsed. Most of them survived.'

'They only had to dig through low density African clay,' said Niall. 'Bolivian clay goes hard as steel when it gets wet.'

'We're trapped,' sobbed Aunty Sue. 'We're all going to suffocate.'

'Calm down, woman,' said Uncle Pete. 'There's enough air in here for hours. We'll drown long before the air runs out.'

Everyone sloshed over to the door and started clawing at it. And kicking it. And trying to smash through it with items of electrical equipment. They kept trying until all Uncle Pete's speakers were floating around them in fragments.

The door didn't budge.

Mum screamed.

Jack knew why. The water was over her waist, and nearly up to his chin.

'Jack,' yelled Mum. 'Hang on to something. Pick him up, somebody.'

Dad grabbed Jack and lifted him up. Jack hadn't realized Dad was so strong. Though now he thought about it, the stationery shop didn't have a forklift, so Dad must get a lot of exercise carrying all the boxes by hand.

'A chair,' said Aunty Sue. 'Get him a chair.'

The adults splashed around for ages until somebody found a chair under the water. Dad carefully helped Jack stand on it.

The water was only up to Jack's waist now.

But it was up to everyone else's chest.

Then the lights went out.

There was quite a lot of shouting and screaming. After a while, Mum yelled at everyone to be quiet, and after another while, they were. Mostly because, as Jack saw in the faint light from Aunty Anthea's phone, which she was holding over her head, the water was up to their chins.

'There must be another way of getting that door open,' spluttered Uncle Rob. 'A mechanical override.'

'There is,' gasped Uncle Pete. 'But it needs a tiny allen key, and the builders lost it.'

Aunty Sue started crying again.

Then Jack had an idea. 'Dad,' he said. 'Have you got a paperclip?'

Dad frowned as he thought about this. 'Paperclip,' he said. 'Paperclip … '

Then his face brightened. 'Yes,' he said. 'One of the

new Ezyglide Antistatics.

I brought it home to show Mum.'

He rummaged around under the water, and Jack guessed he was going through his pockets.

'Please,' murmured Aunty Anthea desperately. 'Please find it.'

Dad raised his hand out of the water.

He was holding a paperclip.

'Thank God,' sobbed Aunty Sue and then gurgled as her mouth filled with water.

Jack watched Dad move slowly towards the door, paperclip held high.

Dad reached the door, took a big breath of air and ducked under the surface of the water.

Jack stood on tiptoe to keep the water away from his mouth and counted the seconds.

Forty.

Fifty.

Sixty and still Dad hadn't come back up.

Jack prayed that correction fluid got spilled a lot in stationery shops. The stuff that gave off pongy fumes. Which meant Dad would have had lots of practice holding his breath.

Seventy.

So he wouldn't drown.

Eighty seconds.

The water level dropped immediately, and the family members screamed and cheered and spluttered and sobbed.

Then the water level stopped going down.

Jack saw why. Outside the door, the steep concrete steps going up to the garden were preventing the rest of the water from flowing away.

But it didn't matter. The door was open now and daylight was coming in, and fresh air, and the distant sound above them of an automatic pool cleaner sucking itself dry in an empty pool.

Suddenly there was a clunk and a gurgle and a loud sucking sound, and the door started to slide open.

And there was Dad, head and shoulders out of the water, staring at the paperclip in his hand with relief and gratitude.

Dad wasn't the only one doing that.

The whole family was gazing at the paperclip that way. And at Dad. And not just with relief and gratitude.

With awe and admiration and respect as well.

Jack grinned, careful to keep his mouth closed because with so much panic somebody was bound to have done a wee in the water.

OK, he said to himself as he swam over to Mum and Dad. *I admit it. Big family get-togethers aren't so bad after all.*

Bovine Espionage

By Jeremy Strong

Harvey was thinking and what Harvey was thinking was: farms stink. They reek of horses and cows and sheep and things that decompose and leave a noxious smell fouling the air. *In fact*, thought Harvey, *they stink of things that stink. Why do there have to be so many malodorous things in one place? On the other hand*, his brain went on, *maybe it's actually better that all the whiffy stuff is in one place because that means there's less stink elsewhere.*

And then again, Harvey wondered, *why did his brain have to think about such boring stuff at all? Why couldn't he think about something interesting, exciting, astonishing, wonderful, strange, bizarre, perplexing or boggling? And why was his brain turning into a thesaurus?*

Harvey carefully skirted round a disgusting spillage that took up half the farmyard and headed for the green and pleasant-looking fields beyond. It had been his father's idea that they should take a week's vacation on a farm.

'Why a farm?' Harvey had asked his dad, and quickly added, 'Does it have a pool?'

'A farm with a swimming pool?' his dad chuckled. 'Can sheep swim? Do chickens go diving?'

Dad often laughed at his own jokes. Nobody else did, least of all Harvey.

'Listen,' said Dad. 'I can't afford Spain or Italy or Disneyland. I've hardly enough dosh to get us to the Isle of Wight. At least we can have a break, together. Somewhere different. There'll be lots to do. You can run around, be free. We'll do stuff.'

Yeah. That's what Dad had said. Now Dad was in the room they were sharing, taking an afternoon nap and snoring. Harvey was outside, being free, but not running around because he was as likely to run into some kind of festering farmyard slop as anything else. Instead he had taken a small pad and a couple of pencils. He thought he might draw something. He liked sketching and it was at least something to do. He headed for the fields and the trees and the sky.

Harvey walked for ten minutes or so along a dirt track, skirting a field which was growing something that wasn't grass but was otherwise unrecognizable. 'Not-grass' was what he called it in his mind, so he thought it better to steer clear in case it was a crop of some sort. He wasn't entirely sure what crops were. They were just a word he'd heard at school. 'Crops grow on farms.' That's what it had said in the book they were reading. Maybe the book had said what kind of crops grew on farms, but Harvey's mind had drifted off somewhere else by then. His mind was always drifting off. It was like a boat with no mooring place and no mooring rope either.

He came to a large field full of cows. They were eating the grass. Were cows a kind of crop, he wondered? After all, they were growing and they were in a field. Harvey sometimes felt his world was so unbearably banal that being daft cheered him up.

The cows were black and white and they looked rather content as they went about hoovering up the grass. Harvey leaned on the gate and watched. Sometimes the cows watched him, glancing up from time to time to see what he was up to, which was in fact nothing.

One cow eventually detached itself from the herd and slowly plodded towards him. Stopping at the gate, the cow considered Harvey for a long time and gave a quiet 'fffff' through its wet nostrils. Finally it raised its head a little.

'Can you write?' The cow's voice was low, slow and rather melancholy.

'Yes,' answered Harvey, somewhat surprised but pleased to chat.

'Then I want you to write some things down for me.'

'Why?' asked Harvey, not unreasonably.

'Because cows can't write,' the cow replied, equally reasonably. 'And I have things to say.'

Harvey got out his sketch pad and pencil. 'Do you have a name?' he asked.

The cow glanced at him moodily, then turned away. 'Buttercup,' she spat. 'Buttercup. What kind of name is that for an MI6 agent? Where's the drama? The action? Adventure? Buttercup, 008 and three quarters, licence to chew.' The cow snorted, or maybe it was a cow-laugh. Harvey wasn't sure.

'You were an MI6 agent?' he repeated.

'Yes.'

'Why should I believe you?' he asked.

'Have you ever heard a cow talk before?'

Evidently this was proof postive, at least to the cow, that mendacity was way beyond her moral boundaries.

Harvey shook his head and thought maybe he should inform Buttercup that this was the first time in his life that he'd actually been near a cow, so he'd not had a chance to chew the cud and swop bovine banter before.

In any case, Buttercup wasn't short of conversation herself and she went on. 'It's not because they can't converse,' sighed the cow. 'It's because they have nothing to say.' She glanced at the chewing herd. 'They're lost in a blissful moo-niverse and live life off pat.' Buttercup frowned for a moment. 'Or maybe that should be on pat. Beside pat? Anyhow', she continued, shaking her head slowly, '*they've* done nothing at all. But *me* – I've had ambitions. Write this down. I was a secret agent for three years, working in the field.'

The cow raised her head and surveyed the field she was in. 'Not *this* field, of course. It's an expression. It means I wasn't working in an office, but outside, on the ground, you know – surveillance.' She said, *sotto voce*.

Harvey's pencil hesitated and the cow shot him a frustrated glance. 'S - U - R - V - E - I -'

'OK,' Harvey interrupted. 'I'm not stupid. What sort of things were you spying on?'

'Nocturnal combine harvester movements.' The cow nodded seriously.

'Are combine harvesters dangerous to national security?' Harvey enquired.

'Very much so, so you can wipe that smirk off your face, young man. Obviously they are not really combine harvesters. They merely look like combine harvesters. Some of them are satellite jamming devices. Some are used for long-distance eavesdropping on spy chatter. And some, SOME are used for harvesting wheat. Just to make it all look tickety-boo. It's called *sheep-dipping*. Of course you won't know what that means. It's an expression used by the CIA. It means that something is rendered to look like something it isn't, so that the something it isn't doesn't know it is. Something. Not the something it isn't. If you get my drift.'

Harvey definitely did not get the cow's drift. In fact, confusion had spread across his face like an unpleasant page full of algebra. He decided it would be a good idea to move on to a different subject. 'But how did you ever come to be a spy in the first place?'

'I was singled out for my intelligence. I got noticed. I think it was when they saw me driving the tractor.'

'You can drive tractors?'

'Not exactly drive it, but I was trying to drive it. I'd seen what you people do with your feet on the pedals and your hands doing this and that and I thought, *I could do that*. Only I couldn't.'

'Oh,' said Harvey. 'Sad. What was the problem?'

'I didn't have the keys.' Buttercup chewed a small piece of turf for a few moments. 'Anyhow, they saw that and took me away to Spy School. Mind-boggling. The things they do! Extraordinary. They were training up all sorts – mice, hedgehogs, frogs, goldfish – almost anything that moved.

Harvey felt the cow was almost smiling as she recalled her past.

'Did you have special gadgets?' he asked.

'I had infra-red night vision spectacles – that was when I was keeping a look-out for illegal combine harvesters. And I had a secret tablet I could take that turned my milk into a very slippery substance. I used that when I was being chased. I'd spray it on the road and the surface would become so slippery cars would skid all over the place. I had mini rockets attached to my hooves that made me gallop at five times normal cow-speed. I loved that. When I wanted to stop I had to deploy a special parachute as a brake, hidden in my tail. I was brilliant at being stealthy and concealing myself. My favourite hiding place was up a tree. Nobody expected to find a cow up a tree, so they never looked!'

'You can climb trees? Wow! That's extraordinary!'

'Thank you,' nodded the cow, visibly pleased. 'It took me a long time to master that particular skill but it was worth it.'

'Could you show me?' Harvey asked. 'I'd love to see you do that.'

'Ah,' murmured the cow. 'Sadly I have arthritis in both my front knees now. That's why I'm in this field, retired. I've been put out to grass, literally! And secondly, I can't show you any of my skills because of the Official Secrets Act, which I had to sign. Sorry.'

Harvey couldn't help being disappointed. He'd been planning to obtain a photo of the cow up a tree so he could show his dad what he'd missed by having an afternoon nap. Buttercup must have sensed Harvey's disappointment because she tried to cheer him up by telling him that she'd been awarded a medal.

'Really? By the Queen?'

'No, not the Queen. The Queen's friend. Look, you can see it. The Queen's friend couldn't pin it on me anywhere so eventually he stuck it to my ear.'

'But isn't that the kind of plastic tag all the cows have?' asked Harvey.

'No, it isn't,' Buttercup said firmly. 'It's a medal. All the other cows have bits of useless plastic hanging off their ears. It's a bling thing and it's ridiculous. I'm the only one with a medal.'

'It looks just like what the other cows have,' Harvey pointed out.

'And you look like just any ordinary stupid kid,' snapped Buttercup. 'I thought you were special but it seems you're not special at all. This medal has been sheep-dipped, like the combine harvesters,' she added petulantly.

'Sorry,' muttered Harvey. 'I do think you are extraordinary.'

But Buttercup had turned away and was staring up the field.

'Really,' Harvey pressed ahead. 'Quite extraordinary.'

The cow trampled the ground a bit with her feet and snorted.

'Exceptional,' Harvey told her. 'Remarkable, singular, phenomenal, fantastic, awesome –'

'All right,' humphed the cow. 'Don't overdo it.' She remained staring at the rest of the herd. 'Look at them. You know what their problem is? They have no imagination. Not a jot. Not an atom. Not even a Higgs Boson.' She paused for a moment before slowly turning back to Harvey.

'Just because I'm a cow doesn't mean I don't have ambitions. I really wanted to be an astronaut. The first cow to walk in space. They didn't give me a chance. They sent a dog up there. They sent a monkey up there. Canines, primates. What do they know? Can they climb trees? Huh!'

Harvey was on the edge of pointing out that monkeys were very good at climbing trees, but after Buttercup's recent outburst he decided to keep his mouth shut.

'I even considered climbing Mount Everest but I hate queueing. Have you seen the queues for the summit recently? Reminded me of the milking parlour, quite beyond the pale. Huh, huh. Anyhow, I'm getting old. Time is running out. Have you got everything down?'

'I think so.'

'Then I'd better get back to the common herd before they think I'm weird or some kind of spy. Ha ha!'

'Will you be here tomorrow?'

'Who can tell?' said the cow, archly. 'Life should be an adventure, don't you think?'

'I do,' agreed Harvey. 'Might see you tomorrow then.'

The cow gave a brief nod and slowly began to make her way back up the field to the rest of the herd.

Harvey headed back to the farmhouse. His father was standing at the door. 'What have you been up to?' he asked.

'Talking to a cow,' Harvey answered.

'Really,' said Dad. 'And what did the cow have to say?'

'That life should be an adventure and it is important to have ambitions.'

'Clever cow,' smirked Dad.

Harvey looked at his father. He loved his dad but didn't think he had ever had an adventure, and ambition for Dad was simply earning a bit more money, that was all. Now Harvey realized he wanted more than that. Where was the drama? The adventure?

Harvey was thinking and this is what he thought: *If a cow can do it, I could do it.*

Pippi Dances with Burglars

By Astrid Lindgren

After Pippi's performance at the circus, there wasn't a single person in the whole little town who didn't know how incredibly strong she was. There was even something about her in the newspaper. But people who lived elsewhere, of course, didn't know who Pippi was.

One dark autumn night, two tramps came trudging along the road past Villa Villekulla. The tramps were two shabby burglars who had set off to roam through the country, looking for things to steal. They saw lights on in the windows of Villa Villekulla, and they decided to go inside and ask for a sandwich.

On that night, Pippi had poured all her gold coins out on the kitchen floor, and she was sitting there counting them. She wasn't actually very good at counting, but occasionally she did it all the same. Just to keep things in order.

' ... seventy-five, seventy-six, seventy-seven, seventy-eight, seventy-nine, seventy-ten, seventy-eleven, seventy-twelve, seventy-thirteen, seventy-seventeen ... I seem to be stuck on seventy! Good gracious, surely there must be some other numbers in the number nebula. Oh, that's right, I remember now: one hundred and four, one thousand. That's certainly a lot of money,' said Pippi.

At that moment someone pounded on the door.

'Come in or stay outside, whatever you like,' yelled Pippi. 'I'm not forcing anybody!'

The door opened and the two tramps came in. Just imagine how big their eyes got when they saw a little red-headed girl sitting on the floor all alone, counting money!

'Are you at home by yourself?' they asked slyly.

'Not at all,' said Pippi. 'Mr Nilsson is at home too.'

The burglars couldn't know, of course, that Mr Nilsson was a little monkey who was asleep in his green-painted bed with a doll's blanket pulled over him. They thought that the master of the house was named Nilsson, and they gave each other a meaningful wink.

Let's come back a little later, was what they meant by that wink. But to Pippi they said, 'Well, we just came in to see what your clock says.'

They were so excited that they forgot all about the sandwiches.

'Big, strong fellows like you, and you don't even know what a clock says?' said Pippi. 'Who brought you up, anyway? Haven't you ever heard a clock before? A clock is a little round *thingamajig* that says "tick tock" and keeps going and going but never gets to the door. If you know any other riddles, let's hear them,' said Pippi, to encourage them.

The tramps thought that Pippi was too young to know about clocks, so without another word they turned on their heels and left.

'I'm not asking you to play tic-tac-toe!' Pippi yelled after them. 'But you could at least play along with my tick-tock riddle. I don't know what makes you tick! But never mind, go in peace,' said Pippi, and she went back to counting her money.

Safely outside, the tramps rubbed their hands with glee.

'Did you see all that money? Good heavens!' said one of them.

'Yeah, we're really in luck,' said the other. 'All we have to do is wait until the girl and that Nilsson go to sleep. Then we'll sneak inside and get our mitts on all that money.'

They sat down under an oak tree in the garden to wait. It was drizzling, and they were very hungry, so it wasn't especially pleasant, but the thought of all that money kept their spirits high.

The lights went out in the other houses, one by one, but in Villa Villekulla the lights stayed on. This was because Pippi was learning to dance a polka, and she didn't want to go to bed until she was positive that she could do it right. But finally the windows in Villa Villekulla also went dark.

The tramps waited quite a while to make sure that Mr Nilsson would be asleep. Finally they sneaked over to the kitchen door and got ready to prise it open with their burglary tools. Then one of them – whose name was Blom, by the way – happened by chance to try the door. It wasn't locked.

'How stupid can people be?' he whispered to his partner. 'Look at this – the door is open!'

'All the better for us,' replied his partner, a black-haired man called Thunder-Karlsson by those who knew him.

Thunder-Karlsson switched on his torch, and then they sneaked into the kitchen. No one was there. The room next to it was Pippi's bedroom, which was also where Mr Nilsson's little doll's bed stood.

Thunder-Karlsson opened the door and cautiously peeked inside. It was nice and quiet, and he let the beam of his torch play over the room.

When the beam came to Pippi's bed, both tramps saw to their surprise that there was nothing but a pair of feet resting on the pillow. As usual, Pippi had her head under the covers at the foot of the bed.

'That must be the girl,' whispered Thunder-Karlsson to Blom. 'And she seems to be sound asleep. But where on earth do you think Nilsson is?'

'Mister Nilsson, if you don't mind,' said Pippi's calm

voice from under the covers. 'Mister Nilsson is sleeping in the little green doll's bed.'

The tramps were so startled that they were just about to rush out. But then they happened to think about what Pippi had said. Mr Nilsson was sleeping in the doll's bed. And in the beam of the torch they caught sight of the doll's bed and the little monkey who was lying in it.

Thunder-Karlsson couldn't help laughing. 'Blom,' he said. 'Mr Nilsson is a monkey. Ha ha ha!'

'Well, what did you think he was?' said Pippi's calm voice from under the covers. 'A lawnmower?'

'Aren't your mamma and pappa home?' asked Blom.

'Nope,' said Pippi. 'They're gone! Gone far away!'

Thunder-Karlsson and Blom were so delighted that they started chuckling.

'Now listen here, little girl,' said Thunder-Karlsson, 'come out of there so we can talk to you!'

'Nope,' said Pippi. 'I'm sleeping. Does this have to do with more riddles? If that's the case, you'll have to answer this one first: what kind of clock goes and goes but never gets to the door?'

Then Blom took a firm grip on the covers and lifted them off.

'Can you dance a polka?' asked Pippi, giving him a serious look. 'I can!'

'You ask too many questions,' said Thunder-Karlsson. 'Why don't you let us ask a few questions now? For instance, where did you put the money that you had out on the floor a while ago?'

'In the suitcase in the cabinet,' replied Pippi truthfully.

Thunder-Karlsson and Blom grinned.

'I hope you won't mind, my dear, if we take it,' said Thunder-Karlsson.

'Oh, not at all,' said Pippi. 'Of course not.'

And with that, Blom went over and took out the suitcase.

'I hope you won't mind, my dear, if I take it back,' said Pippi, as she climbed out of bed and went over to Blom.

Blom didn't really know what happened, but somehow the suitcase suddenly ended up in Pippi's hand.

'Quit joking around,' said Thunder-Karlsson angrily. 'Give me that suitcase!'

He grabbed Pippi hard by the arm and tried to yank

the plunder away from her.

'Who says I was joking?' said Pippi as she lifted Thunder-Karlsson on top of the cabinet. The next instant Blom was sitting there too. Then both of the tramps were scared. They began to realize that Pippi was not exactly an ordinary girl. But the suitcase was still tempting them, so they pushed aside their fear.

'All together now, Blom,' shouted Thunder-Karlsson, and then they jumped down from the cabinet and rushed at Pippi, who was holding the suitcase in her hand. But Pippi jabbed them with her finger and they each landed in opposite corners of the room. Before they could get to their feet, Pippi got out a rope, and quick as a wink she tied up the arms and legs of both burglars. Now they started singing a different tune.

'My dear, sweet little girl,' pleaded Thunder-Karlsson. 'Please forgive us. We were only joking! Don't hurt us. We're just a couple of poor tramps who came in to ask for a little food.'

Blom even managed to shed a few tears.

Pippi put the suitcase back in its place in the cabinet. Then she turned to face her prisoners. 'Can either of you dance a polka?'

'Hmm ... well ... ' said Thunder-Karlsson. 'I suppose we both can.'

'Oh, what fun!' said Pippi, clapping her hands. 'Couldn't we dance for a bit? I've just learned how, you see.'

'Er ... of course,' said Thunder-Karlsson, rather surprised.

Then Pippi got out a big pair of scissors and cut off the ropes that were holding her visitors.

'But we don't have any music,' said Pippi anxiously.

Then she had an idea. 'Could you blow on a comb?' she said to Blom. 'Then I'll dance with him.' And she pointed to Thunder-Karlsson.

Yes, of course, Blom could blow on a comb. And that's what he did, so loudly that it could be heard through the whole house.

Mr Nilsson was startled awake, and he sat up in bed just in time to see Pippi whirling around with Thunder-Karlsson. Her expression was dead serious, and she was dancing with such energy, as if her life depended on it.

Finally Blom refused to blow on the comb any more because he claimed that it was tickling his lips so terribly. And Thunder-Karlsson's legs were starting to get tired since he'd been trudging along the road all day long.

'Oh please, just a little bit more,' begged Pippi as she kept on dancing. And there was nothing for Blom and Thunder-Karlsson to do but keep going.

When it was three in the morning, Pippi said, 'Oh, I could keep on like this until Thursday! But maybe you're tired or hungry?'

That was exactly what they were, although they hardly dared say so. From the pantry Pippi brought out bread and cheese and butter and ham and a cold roast and milk, and then they all sat down at the table – Blom and Thunder-Karlsson and Pippi – and they ate until they were stuffed to the gills.

Pippi poured a little milk in one ear. 'It's good for an earache,' she said.

'You poor thing. Do you have an earache?' asked Blom.

'Nope,' said Pippi. 'But I might get one.'

Finally both tramps stood up, thanked Pippi for the food, and said that they would have to be going.

'I'm so glad you came! Do you really have to leave so soon?' said Pippi sadly.

'I've never seen anyone who can dance a polka like you can, my sweet little sugar pig,' she said to Thunder-Karlsson.

'And be sure to keep practising at playing the comb,' she told Blom. 'Then you won't notice that it tickles.'

As they headed out of the door, Pippi came running to give each of them a gold coin. 'You've certainly earned it,' she said.

Jacqueline's Moon

By Josephine Feeney

In the summer of 1969 my best friend was Jacqueline
Richards. Jacqueline was a very popular name in
those days – there were five of them in my class. They
were all named after a famous lady called Jacqueline
Kennedy. But my Jacqueline was the best. She was
brilliant at double-ball, handstands, inventing new
games and writing stories. She was a faithful friend.

    I longed for the start of the big summer holidays
in 1969 so that I could play out all day with my
Jacqueline. My mum had other ideas. The first day
of the long holidays, Mum said, 'Lydia, your fringe is
getting in your eyes. Shall we go to Mr Carlyle?' I knew
by the way that she'd said my name that this wasn't a
question – it was an order.

I didn't want to go. 'I'm trying to grow it,' I said, peeping at Mum from one side of my fringe.

'It's a mess, Lydia,' Mum said.

'I know, but when it gets a bit longer I'll be able to tie it back …'

'If that's all you want to do, you might as well get it cut.'

'I hate Mr Carlyle's …'

'Don't be difficult, Lydia.'

Mr Carlyle had his hairdressing shop in between the garage and Mrs Oxton's, the bakery. He talked and talked. He was always talking. He never even stopped to ask what style you wanted. He had only one style for girls and one for boys.

The hairdressing shop was like an ordinary house with a big window. Mr Carlyle had two big chairs in his front room and a small sink underneath a huge, round mirror. In one corner there was a pile of towels. He wrapped one round my neck. I stared at my reflection in the window.

'What's it to be today?' he asked brightly.

'Cut please, Mr Carlyle,' Mum replied. 'Nice and

short. I don't want it in her eyes for the holidays,' she continued.

'Right,' Mr Carlyle said. When Mum settled on the other chair and started to flick through a magazine, Mr Carlyle asked, 'How's your friend Jacqueline, then?'

'She's very well, thank you.'

My mum was watching me as I spoke.

'It's a great time to be young,' Mr Carlyle stated.

I never knew what to say when grown-ups said things like that.

'Yes,' Mum agreed.

'When I was young,' Mr Carlyle began, 'there were no houses past Claypit Road. It was all fields. Have I told you this before?'

He had. Every time I'd been for a haircut. In fact, me and Jacqueline sometimes pretended to be Mr Carlyle and we used to say, 'When I was young ... '

'Yes, it was all fields. A grand place for playing out, but the youngsters didn't get much chance for playing in them days,' Mr Carlyle went on. 'No, we always had to be running errands. That's what I mean when I say, it's a great time to be young. How short do you want this fringe, Mrs Porter?'

'Nice and short, Mr Carlyle. We don't want it getting in her eyes during the holidays, do we, Lydia?' Mum said, smiling at Mr Carlyle.

'No,' I said, although it didn't matter what I said anyway.

'Take the moon, Mrs Porter,' Mr Carlyle continued. 'Youngsters have got all that to look forward to ... I mean, they're setting off tonight, aren't they, from America and then they're going to land on the moon and walk on it. I was watching it last night –'

'Waste of money, if you ask me,' Mum said, hardly glancing up from her magazine.

'Oh no, oh no, Mrs Porter – you can't say that. I'll bet any money, by the year 1980 people will be going to the moon on holiday!' Mr Carlyle said. He was so excited with all this moon talk that he cut my fringe very badly. 'Oops, Lydia, just have to straighten it up a bit.'

Mr Carlyle cut my fringe really short. I knew Jacqueline would laugh as soon as she saw it. I felt very angry. I could hardly answer Mr Carlyle when he asked, 'Will you be watching, then, on the telly, Lydia?'

'I hate Mr Carlyle,' I said angrily, when me and Mum arrived back home.

'Lydia!' Mum said in her warning voice. 'Don't say you hate anyone.'

'Well, I do – look at the mess he's made of my hair,' I said.

'It'll grow, Lydia. He's a very experienced hairdresser, Mr Carlyle. He used to cut my hair when I was a girl,' Mum said. 'So if it was good enough for me … '

'You see, if he's that old, Mum, he shouldn't be cutting people's hair. He could be dangerous … '

'Don't be cheeky, Lydia,' Mum hissed.

I didn't mean to be cheeky.

'You're not playing out with Jacqueline if you're going to be cheeky.'

'I don't want to play with anyone. They'll laugh at my fringe,' I said quietly. But when Jacqueline called for me, she didn't even notice my fringe.

'Guess what?' she said. She stared right at me.

I couldn't think of anything to say.

'You'll never guess, I'll tell you. You know Terence Keane? His mum and dad have got a new telly and it's colour!'

'Colour?'

'Yeah – and guess what else? He said we can all go and watch it tonight, watch the children's programmes.'

'Tonight?'

'Yeah, well, about five o'clock, and Terence's mum said we can bring our mums and dads too, if they want to come.'

My mum didn't want to go. She said, 'You can't make the news any better just because it's colour.'

Everyone, apart from my mum, was there. Even Mr Carlyle was in Terence's front room.

'I'll be interested to see what the moon looks like in colour,' Mr Carlyle said.

'He's mad on the moon,' I whispered to Jacqueline. 'He kept on about it today when ... '

'I thought your face looked a bit funny,' Jacqueline said. 'It's your hair, isn't it? Still, at least you've got six weeks for your fringe to grow.' She was kind, my Jacqueline.

'Jacqueline, I'm sure you don't talk like this when you're at the pictures,' Mrs Keane said. 'If you did you'd get thrown out.'

'Sorry, Mrs Keane,' Jacqueline said.

It was like being at the pictures, sitting in Terence's front room, staring at a colour television, even if it was all about the moon. It wasn't a real colour television, the sort we have now. No, it had a sort of plastic colour screen over the front of the television to make the black and white pictures more colourful. Mr Keane had brought it back from his aunt in Ireland.

'If you like,' Mr Keane said without moving his eyes from the television, 'you can all come and watch when they land on the moon.'

'That's very kind of you,' Mr Carlyle said. 'I'll look forward to that.'

'We could make some sandwiches and have a bit of a party,' Mrs Keane said.

'Good idea,' Mr Keane said. 'Let's have a party!'

For the next few days, everyone on the street was talking about the moon and the Keanes' new television.

Jacqueline and I played double-ball against the Painters' huge, iron garage door.

'Are you going to the telly party, Lid?'

'Are you, Jack?'

We always called one another shortened names when we played double-ball. Otherwise it was too hard to concentrate.

'No. Mum wants to go, so I'll have to stay and look after the little 'uns,' Jacqueline said.

'I'm not going if you're not going, Jack.'

Then Mr Painter started to wind up his garage door.

'Will you girls go and play down your own end!' he shouted. 'You're giving me a headache.'

Jacqueline and I stood and stared at Mr Painter.

'Well, go on, then. Clear off down your own end!' he shouted.

We walked slowly away. I had thought about answering him back, but I knew he'd march me home if I did that. I looked back to see him watching as we turned the corner into Jacqueline's entry. There was nowhere else as good as Mr Painter's garage for playing double-ball.

Jacqueline stared down at her tennis ball. 'Why is

everybody watching it on the telly?'

'Watching what?'

'The moon.'

'I don't know,' I said, shrugging my shoulders.

'I mean, it's only up there, isn't it?' Jacqueline pointed up towards the sky.

'Yes.'

'Well, why don't we watch it ourselves?'

'Do you mean on your telly?' I asked.

'No! We've got a brilliant view of the moon from our attic. I watch it all the time. I can see all the mountains and lakes … '

'Have you got a telescope, then?'

'No, I use my dad's binoculars, but you're nearer to the moon when you're in the attic,' Jackie replied enthusiastically. 'I'll go and ask Mum if you can come and stay with us.'

'What about my mum?' I shouted after Jacqueline, but she didn't hear me – she was running across her back yard and into the back door. 'Mam! Mam!' she shouted.

I followed her, knocked on the back door and, when nobody answered, walked quietly into the kitchen. Jacqueline's dad sat at the kitchen table, reading the paper.

'How are you, Lydia?' Jacqueline's dad asked.

'Fine thanks, Mr Richards,' I said. He looked back at his paper. 'Jack's come to see about the moon, watching the moon,' I said, by way of explanation.

'I hear the Keanes have a new television. Have you seen it yet?' Mr Richards asked.

Before I had a chance to answer, Jacqueline ran into the room. 'You can! If your mum says it's all right, you can stay here for the night and we can watch the moon!'

On 20 July 1969, Neil Armstrong and Edwin Aldrin Jnr became the first men to walk on the moon. Me and Jacqueline watched from the attic bedroom of 23 Swan Street. We took it in turns to look through the binoculars. While the rest of the world watched it on television, or on cinema screens, me and Jacqueline sat on the attic bedroom windowsill, with heavy black binoculars glued to our eyes.

When it was Jacqueline's turn with the binoculars, I looked down at the front room of Terence's house. Shadows seemed to jump out of the house and people stood on the doorstep, desperate for a view of the amazing happenings.

'Can you see anything?' I asked Jacqueline for the hundredth time.

'Don't keep asking!' Jacqueline replied impatiently. She was a bit impatient at times, my Jacqueline. But we can't all be perfect – that's what my mum says.

'Where's the moon?' I said quietly. I didn't want to upset Jacqueline.

'I'm not sure – it might be round the back of the earth, which means it'll probably show up in a few minutes.'

'And will we be able to see them then?' I asked hopefully.

'Oh yes,' Jacqueline said. 'They'll only look like matchstick men with a little blob for the buggy but we'll see them, don't worry.'

'It's very historic, isn't it, Jacqueline?'

'That's what Mr Carlyle says!' Jacqueline said, handing me the binoculars and laughing.

Just at that very moment, the clouds raced across the sky and the moon appeared. Jacqueline snatched the binoculars back. 'Told you, told you the moon was round the back of Earth!'

'But it's my turn, Jacqueline,' I pleaded.

'Oh, all right, then, have a quick go,' she conceded.

After a moment, Jacqueline took the binoculars back and held them tightly to her face. For ages she didn't say anything, then suddenly, 'I can see them, Lydia! I can see them!'

'Who?' I asked, forgetting, for a moment, our true purpose in the attic.

'The moon men!' Jacqueline snapped.

'What do they look like?' I whispered.

'Matchstick men, but it's them ... hang on a minute, I think they're shaking hands. Yes! They are, they're shaking hands!'

'Can I have a look?'

She reluctantly handed over the binoculars. I peered through them. I couldn't see a thing.

'Whereabouts are they, Jack? I can't see anything.'

She snatched the binoculars back again. 'You're not used to these, that's why you can't see through them. They're sort of in the middle, next to a kind of crater. If you'd got good eyesight and you knew how to use these binocs, then you'd be able to see them.' She stared into the glasses again. 'They're like matchstick men with big bubbles on their heads – that's their helmets. See if you can see them now, Lydia.'

'Oh yes … ' I said quietly. 'In the middle. Are there two or three?'

'Two. You're not just saying that, are you, Lydia?'

'What?' I asked, surprised.

'You're not just *pretending* that you can see them, are you?' Jacqueline asked, like a suspicious adult.

'No, I can see them – only it's hard if you're wearing spectacles too,' I said, handing the binoculars back.

'This is historic, Lid. Watching the men on the moon. I think they've gone into their car now,' Jacqueline said.

'I thought they had a rocket, Jack,' I said.

'Yes, but they took a car in the rocket – Dad told me. He read it in the paper today.'

'Must've been a big rocket! Where did they park it?' I asked.

'Round the corner,' Jacqueline said confidently. She had grown into a moon expert. 'The other man's in it. He's keeping it going while these two walk around … just in case they have to get away quickly. Do you want to have another look?' Jacqueline asked.

'No,' I said. 'I'd rather listen while you tell me what's happening.'

'OK,' Jacqueline said, settling into her space on the windowsill.

As she talked and talked about the men on the moon, I realized where I'd heard that tone of voice before. When she had to look after her little 'uns and they asked for a story, that's just what she sounded like.

Jacqueline was brilliant at telling stories and that's why I was happy up there in her attic, watching Jacqueline's moon. It was much better than the real thing.

About the authors

Simon Cheshire loves writing for children because you can fill the stories with mad detectives, robot camels, alien invasions – all the fun stuff that you usually have to leave out of books for adults.

Sir Terry Pratchett is one of the greatest ever writers of funny fantasy stories. He is probably best known for the *Discworld* series. His novel *Truckers* started life as the story in this collection, *Rincemangle, the Gnome of Even Moor.*

Morris Gleitzman is one of Australia's most successful authors. He started by writing films and TV scripts, but then discovered you can get closer to a character's thoughts and feelings in a book than in a film.

Jeremy Strong says he has the best job ever! He spends most of his time writing and visiting schools, libraries and festivals. He is the author of many hilarious best-selling books, including *The Hundred-Mile-An-Hour Dog* and *Krazy Kow Saves the World!*

Astrid Lindgren (1907–2002) was a Swedish writer whose works have been translated into 95 different languages! Pippi Longstocking is probably the most famous of her characters.

Josephine Feeney loves writing stories about family life for children. She knows a lot about it, because she's the fifth child in a family of eight!